NANCY E. KRULIK

SCHOLASTIC INC.
New York Toronto London Auckland Sydney

ISBN 0-590-48086-3
Copyright ©1994 by National Broadcasting Company. SAVED BY THE BELL™ is a trademark of National Broadcasting Company. All rights reserved. Published by Scholastic Inc.

Book design by Dawn Antoniello

12 11 10 9 8 7 6 5 4 3 2 1   4 5 6 7 8/9

Printed in the U.S.A.   14

First Scholastic printing, January 1994

ZACK

I can't believe it! I finally graduated from high school! Me! Zack Morris. But that's not the most unbelievable part. The *most unbelievable* part is that I think I am actually going to miss Bayside High.

For some reason my old principal, Mr. Belding, asked *me* to talk to this new kid, Scott Erickson. Scott's just transferred to Bayside from Valley High, and he's not exactly a "model" student. Seems he's already pulling all kinds of scams — and making money while he's at it!

Sounds just like a chip off *my* old block! Come to think of it, maybe *that's* why Mr. Belding wanted *me* to fill him in on what to expect at Bayside...

Well, I'm always willing to help out Mr. Belding, so I've gathered together some of my old Bayside pals and fellow graduates to help, too. Let me tell you — that was no easy job. Screech was here in California. But Jessie and Lisa were all the way in New York. Kelly was off somewhere — *shopping*!

Still, it was worth all of those *collect* phone calls to get the old gang together, because I think we can convince Scott that Bayside is a pretty cool school.

JESSIE

▌ I learned a lot of things during my four years at Bayside, but I learned my most important lesson on graduation day. You see, just before graduation Mr. Belding told me that I had the highest grade point average in the whole school! That made me valedictorian, which was something I had wanted my *whole* life.

But as it turned out, I *didn't* have the highest grade point average at all — my friend Screech did. Screech knew how much I wanted to be valedictorian, and he asked Mr. Belding to give me the honor.

Screech taught me all about generosity and humility that day.

SCREECH

I just did what any friend would have done. And I learned how to be a friend from the best friend any guy could have — Zack. Even when other kids thought I was a dweeb, Zack never dumped me.

Too bad Zack didn't learn as much as I did at Bayside. But maybe that's because I always did his homework for him!

I have to admit that, for a long time, I thought Screech was a dorky guy. But after the nice thing he did for Jessie, I think the world would be a better place if it had more dorks like Screech.

Uh, I really meant that as a compliment, Screech!

KELLY

Boo hoo! I'll miss Bayside so much. I made so many friends. And I loved everyone so much.

Sob! I think I'll even miss the nerds!

SLATER

Hey Scott, I am the right person to talk to when it comes to being the new kid in school. I speak from experience. See, my dad was in the military, and we moved around a lot.

Thanks to my friends at Bayside, this was the first school I ever felt at home in. I hope you feel the same way some day.

Thanks, gang! You see, Scott, Bayside is more than just a high school. The kids here are kind of like a family. When graduation day finally came for me, I thought it would be the happiest day ever! But then I realized how much I would miss everyone (including all 86 of my girlfriends!). Because the friends you make here at Bayside are the kinds of people who will always be there when you need them.

But you'll find that out yourself! I just hope it doesn't take you until *your* graduation.

MR. BELDING

Well, Scott. I hope Zack and his friends have given you an idea about what life here at Bayside is all about. And if you need anything else, just ask me— your friendly neighborhood principal.

SCOTT

Oh, of course, Mr. Belding. And may I say that is a lovely tie you're wearing.

I guess making friends is important and all that, but—just between us—I know that the real secret to success in high school is hanging with the...

BABES!

▌ may not have been in this school very long, but I've already scoped out the hottest girls: Vicki, Lindsay, and Megan.

MEGAN

Megan is the biggest brain at Bayside High. In fact, I heard a rumor that she was actually *reading* books over summer vacation! *Reading—for fun!* Can you believe it?

VICKI

Vicki is Megan's best friend. And she's kind of okay to talk to — unless you start the conversation with, "How are you?"

That's when Vicki will start to tell you about every health hazard known to man — like how the paint in the bathrooms is bad for you, and how eating a tuna sandwich can kill you because everyone knows that the ocean is a "floating garbage dump."

Vicki is kind of cute, and I hear she's pretty crazy about me. But I only have eyes for one girl at Bayside. And that's . . .

LINDSAY

Beautiful, dark-haired Lindsay... She's in my Lit class. It's the only class I look forward to all day.

Lindsay isn't just beautiful. She's smart, and popular, and really friendly. There's just one problem with Lindsay. *She's going steady.* And her boyfriend isn't some nerd. He's Tommy DeLuca — one of the toughest guys at Bayside!

TOMMY DELUCA

Most people know him better as Tommy D.

He's sometimes seen roaming the halls at Bayside — serving up some "knuckle sandwiches."

If he's not there, he's serving up pizzas at the Max.

Love that hat, Tommy D.!

Sometimes it seems like all Lindsay and Tommy D. do is fight.

I guess that's because making up is so much fun for them.

Don't worry. Someday I'll figure out a way to get between them!

WEASEL

. . . Then again, it just may be a case for Dr. Love!

Dr. Love's secret identity is Weasel Wyzell. Weasel is pretty much of a nerd, but he's my pal.

When I became head of the student radio station, KVIB, I got the idea for Weasel to start giving romantic advice.

Of course, no one would take advice from a geek like Weasel, so I gave him the name Dr. Love.

Dr. Love sure was a hit with the babes!

Let me show you a little bit of what life is *really* like at this school. Sometimes, the classes here at Bayside can actually put you to sleep

To get the real feel of the school, you've got to hang out in the halls.

You wouldn't believe some of the stuff Weasel keeps in his locker!

Check out those dumb bells!

Let's face it—the football team is certainly lacking something in the brains department. The lights are on, but no one's home... if ya know what I mean!

Bayside might not be as cool as Zack says it is, but there is a great hangout nearby. It's called the Max.

It's the kind of place where even a nerd can belt a tune with the karaoke machine!

The food's pretty decent, too!

No spoon is clean enough for picky Vicki!

Yee ha!

And on Western night, the Max is mighty fine, pardner!

'Maybe there *is* something more to high school than babes—like being one of the guys! NAH!

Come to think of it . . . you were right, Zack. I think I *am* going to like it here!